MOVE
On Up That
Beanstalk, Jack!

The Fairy-Tale Physics of Forces and Motion

by Thomas Kingsley Troupe

illustrated by Jomike Tejido

PICTURE WINDOW BOOKS
a capstone imprint

Some time ago, in a land you'll never find on a map, lived a boy named Jack and a mom named Mom. They shared a small house and a sad, empty garden.

"I'm so hungry, I could eat my shoes," Jack said.

"I'm hungry too," Mom said. "I'd make a dirt sandwich, but we're out of bread."

One afternoon, Jack looked out the window at their bony cow named Gloria. She mooed and ate the last pea in the garden. Jack's stomach rumbled.

"We have to do something," he told Mom, "or we're going to starve!"

Gloria stuck out her tongue and swished her tail.

"That's it," Jack said. "I'm going to town to sell that awful cow!"

"Good idea," Mom said, staring at the blank TV screen. "Then we can pay our cable bill."

Jack groaned. "No, we need to buy *food*, Mom."

"Oh, of course," she replied. "Sorry."

Jack went outside, grabbed Gloria's rope, and pulled. The cow wouldn't budge.

"Moo," she said.

"How about you *moo-ve* instead?" Jack said.

"How's it going, Jack?" Mom called from the window.

"I'm pulling on the rope, using a force, but this annoying cow is just standing here," Jack replied.

"A force can be a pull *or* a push," Mom said. "Try pushing her. She'll move."

Jack pushed Gloria as hard as he could. With a grunt, she finally moved, and the two headed to town.

In town, people crowded the streets. They hurried from place to place. Not one of them wanted to buy a bony cow.

"Moo," Gloria said.

"Yeah, we need *moo-ney*," Jack said. "For food. And cable TV."

Just as Jack was ready to give up, he spotted a man selling cell phones and beans. Jack accidentally bumped into the man's table, and some beans fell onto the sidewalk.

"Oops," Jack said. "Sorry about that."

"No problem," the man said. "That's what gravity does!"

"Gravy?" Jack asked. "That sounds delicious right now."

"No," the man said. "Not gravy, *gravity.* It's the force that pulls everything with mass toward Earth's center. Buildings, cars, people . . ."

"I thought things just fell," Jack said.

"*Gravity* makes that happen," the man explained. "Hey, would you like to trade me your cow for these beans?"

"I don't like beans," Jack said.

"Oh, but these are *magic* beans," the man said. "Plant them and you'll grow one amazing, giant-sized—"

"Yeah, OK, sure," Jack said.

Jack couldn't wait to tell his mom the good news.

"Mom! Look!" Jack cried. "I got some beans!"

"We don't like beans," Mom said. "How much money did you get for the cow?"

"No money," Jack said. "Just these beans. *Magic* beans."

"Jack, beans only grow more beans," Mom said. She snatched them from her son's hand and threw them out the window. Hard. The tiny veggies disappeared in the garden dirt.

"Good arm, Mom," Jack said.

"Thank you," Mom said. "That *was* a lot of force, wasn't it?"

Late that night, a thunderstorm soaked the land with rain—and something happened in the garden.

"What is *that*?" Jack cried, looking out the window the next morning. He leapt from bed and raced outside. Mom followed.

A huge, thick beanstalk towered overhead. It stretched high into the clouds.

"Great," Mom said. "Now we'll have tons of giant beans we won't eat."

"I'll try to shake some loose," Jack said. He pushed on the beanstalk . . . and then pushed harder.

The beanstalk wouldn't budge.

Jack gazed at the clouds. Maybe, just maybe, there was something to eat up there. He grabbed his gloves, gave his mom a hug, and started to climb.

He climbed pretty high. And then he climbed some more. After he climbed awhile, he, of course, did some additional climbing. Jack's house down below looked like a tiny speck.

"If I let go right now," he said, "gravity would pull me down. Fast. And that would hurt."

"Hey!" a voice boomed above Jack's head. "What are you doing, little guy?"

Jack froze.

"You look hungry, kid," the voice continued. "Come on up. I'll fix you a sandwich."

Jack had no idea whose voice it was. *But I am pretty hungry*, he thought. *How can I say no to a sandwich?*

So, with a loudly growling stomach, Jack climbed to the top of the beanstalk.

Everything above the clouds was big. Really big. Especially
the man sitting beside the beanstalk.

"Hey, kid," the giant boomed. "I'm Dennis."

"I'm Jack," Jack said.

"Please, enjoy this sandwich!" Dennis said. "It's going to stay
at rest until you eat it."

Jack raised an eyebrow. "Um . . . a sandwich at rest?" he asked.

"It's all about inertia," Dennis said. "Newton's First Law of
Motion says that objects will stay at rest (or in motion) until acted
upon by a force. The 'force' in this case is you!"

"Who's Norton?" Jack asked.

"*Newton.* Sir Isaac *Newton,*" Dennis said. "He studied how objects move. Newton used his discoveries to create the Three Laws of Motion."

"So if I eat some of this delicious-looking sandwich, I'll disrupt its rest?" Jack asked.

"That's right," Dennis said.

"Well, then let's wake it up!" Jack said, tearing off a fistful of bread.

In surprisingly little time, Jack ate a big chunk of the sandwich. "So, Dennis," he asked, "are you a chef?"

"No," the giant said. "I'm studying to be a science teacher. I like figuring out how stuff works."

Jack pointed at the beanstalk. "That thing grew overnight from four magic beans," he said. "It's impossible to move. I tried."

"That's Newton's Second Law of Motion," Dennis said. He showed Jack a page from the physics book in his lap. "An object's speed can change based on its mass and the forces acting upon it."

"The beanstalk didn't move at *all* when I pushed on it," Jack said.

"Right, that's because the beanstalk has a much greater mass compared to you, little guy," Dennis said. "The more mass an object has, the more force is needed to move it. Now, if *I* tried . . ."

Dennis reached over and gave the huge beanstalk a tap. It wobbled.

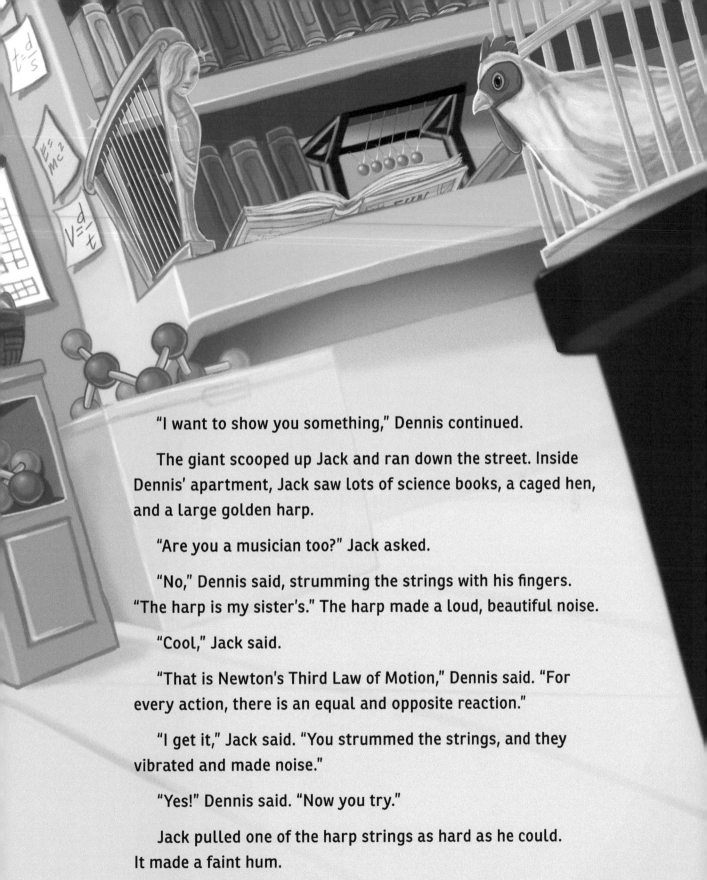

"I want to show you something," Dennis continued.

The giant scooped up Jack and ran down the street. Inside Dennis' apartment, Jack saw lots of science books, a caged hen, and a large golden harp.

"Are you a musician too?" Jack asked.

"No," Dennis said, strumming the strings with his fingers. "The harp is my sister's." The harp made a loud, beautiful noise.

"Cool," Jack said.

"That is Newton's Third Law of Motion," Dennis said. "For every action, there is an equal and opposite reaction."

"I get it," Jack said. "You strummed the strings, and they vibrated and made noise."

"Yes!" Dennis said. "Now you try."

Jack pulled one of the harp strings as hard as he could. It made a faint hum.

"Big strum, big sound. Little strum, little sound," Jack said.

19

Dennis' stomach rumbled and made the kitchen table shake. "You know, Jack," he said with a smile, "it's been a long time since I had a human for lunch."

"Um . . . what do you mean?" Jack asked.

"I mean, it's been a long time since I had company for lunch. It's nice," the giant explained, his stomach rumbling again.

"Oh," Jack said. "So how about a sandwich?"

"I'd love an omelet," Dennis said. "But my hen lays only golden eggs now. Sadly, you can't cook those."

Dennis picked up an egg and tossed it—**THUNK!**—in a basket nearly filled with other golden eggs.

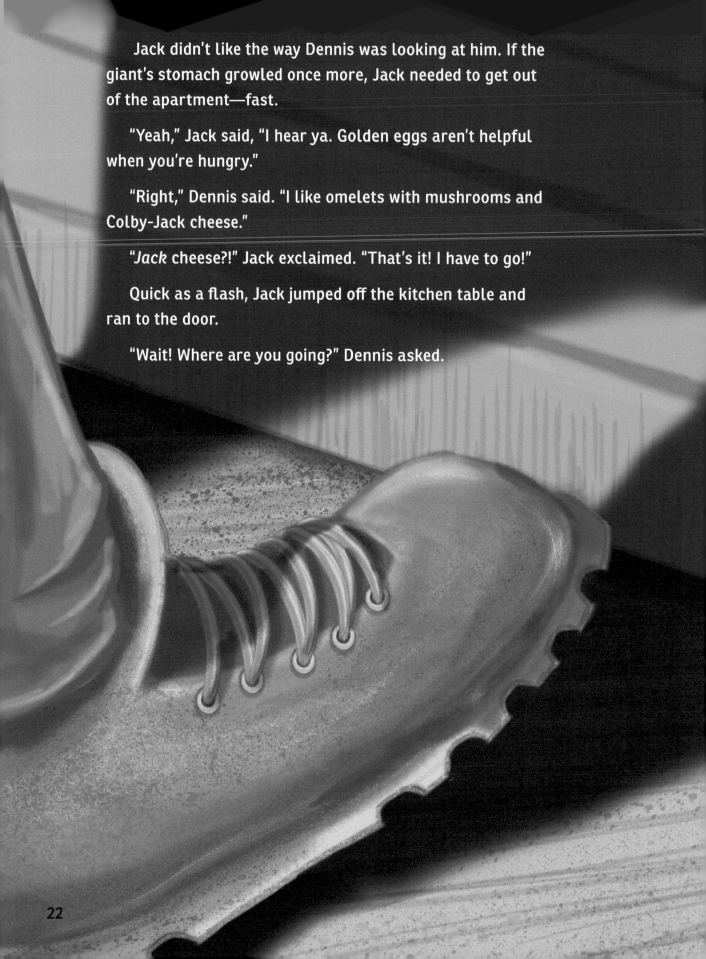

Jack didn't like the way Dennis was looking at him. If the giant's stomach growled once more, Jack needed to get out of the apartment—fast.

"Yeah," Jack said, "I hear ya. Golden eggs aren't helpful when you're hungry."

"Right," Dennis said. "I like omelets with mushrooms and Colby-Jack cheese."

"*Jack* cheese?!" Jack exclaimed. "That's it! I have to go!"

Quick as a flash, Jack jumped off the kitchen table and ran to the door.

"Wait! Where are you going?" Dennis asked.

Jack pushed and pushed, but the door didn't budge. *Oh no,* he thought. *Not another one of Newton's Laws of Motion!*

"Fee, Fi, Fo, *Full*!" Dennis sang, walking up behind him. "This door opens with a *pull*!"

The giant pulled open the door, and Jack scrambled out.

"Hey, wait! What's your hurry, Jack? You forgot your—" Dennis shouted.

"Newton should have a *Fourth* Law of Motion," Jack cried, running as fast as he could. "Anyone chased by a hungry giant will move *really* fast!"

When Jack reached the beanstalk, he tightened his gloves and started sliding down. The giant followed.

"Gloves are a good idea, little guy," Dennis said. "They provide friction. Friction is what happens when the surface of one object meets another."

"How do you *know* all this stuff?" Jack cried.

"Friction can help slow you down," Dennis said. "It works in the opposite direction of motion. Please slow down so I can—"

"Forget it," Jack said. "No way! I don't want to be the cheese in your omelet!"

Jack continued to slide toward home. The whole beanstalk shook as Dennis climbed down after him.

When Jack reached the ground, he yelled toward the house. "Mom! Get an ax! There's a giant coming down the beanstalk after me!"

A moment later, Mom ran out and tossed him an ax.

"Wait, Jack!" Dennis shouted from above.

Jack started to chop. He chopped a lot. And then he chopped some more. After a countless number of chops, he, of course, did some additional chopping.

The beanstalk tipped, then toppled over.

Dennis landed. **BOOM!** Nearby houses collapsed.
A lake spilled into a valley. Somewhere a baby cried.

"Wow! What a drop! Thank goodness my shirt was loose and slowed down my fall," Dennis said. "It created drag, which acted in the opposite direction of motion—kind of like a parachute."

Jack sighed. "Yes, thank goodness," he said. "Well, go ahead and eat me. Get it over with. You wanted to eat me, right? That's why you were chasing me."

"No!" Dennis said. "You dropped your wallet at my apartment. Here."

Jack sheepishly took the wallet from the giant's hand. "Oh," he said in a very, very small voice.

Dennis smiled and asked, "What's for lunch, little guy?"

And so, stuck with a giant mouth to feed, Jack and Mom lived hungrily ever after. However, they did learn a lot about science.

Glossary

drag—the force created when air strikes a moving object; drag slows down moving objects

force—a push or a pull

friction—a force created when two objects rub together; friction slows down moving objects

gravity—a force that pulls objects with mass together

inertia—a property of matter that makes objects resist changes in motion

law—a statement in science about what always happens when certain events take place

mass—the amount of material in an object

motion—movement

physics—the science that deals with matter and energy; physics includes the study of light, heat, sound, electricity, motion, and force

vibrate—to move back and forth quickly

Critical Thinking Questions

1. A force is a push or a pull. Give at least three examples from this story of a force in action.

2. Explain Newton's First Law of Motion using an object from your backpack.

3. Which would be harder for you: to push a baby stroller or a full-size car? Why? Use Newton's Second Law of Motion to explain your answer.

Read More

Barnham, Kay. *Isaac Newton*. Science Biographies. Chicago: Raintree, 2014.

Troupe, Thomas Kingsley. *Are Bowling Balls Bullies?: Learning About Forces and Motion with the Garbage Gang.* The Garbage Gang's Super Science Questions. North Mankato, Minn.: Picture Window Books, a Capstone imprint, 2016.

Winterberg, Jenna. *Balanced and Unbalanced Forces.* Huntington Beach, Calif.: Teacher Created Materials, 2015.

Internet Sites

Use FactHound to find Internet sites related to this book.

Visit *www.facthound.com*

Just type in 9781515828945 and go.

Look for all the books in the series!

Index

Special thanks to our adviser, Darsa Donelan, Professor of Physics,
Gustavus Adolphus College, Saint Peter, Minnesota, for her expertise.

Editor: Jill Kalz
Designer: Lori Bye
Premedia Specialist: Tori Abraham
The illustrations in this book were created digitally.

Picture Window Books
1710 Roe Crest Drive
North Mankato, MN 56003
www.mycapstone.com

Library of Congress Cataloging-in-Publication data is available on the Library of Congress website.
ISBN 978-1-5158-2894-5 (library binding)
ISBN 978-1-5158-2898-3 (paperback)
ISBN 978-1-5158-2902-7 (eBook PDF)
Summary: When times are tough, you pull yourself up and push yourself to the top . . . of a beanstalk . . .
where you might get schooled in forces and motion by a STEM-loving giant named Dennis. At least that's
what happens to Jack in this delicious twist on a classic fairy tale.

Printed in the United States   4735